The Jury Duty

US Government and Politics
Children's Government Books

BABY PROFESSOR
EDUCATION KIDS

Speedy Publishing LLC

40 E. Main St. #1156

Newark, DE 19711

www.speedypublishing.com

Copyright 2017

In this book, we're going to cover how jury duty works and why it's an important part of our legal system in the United States. Let's get right to it!

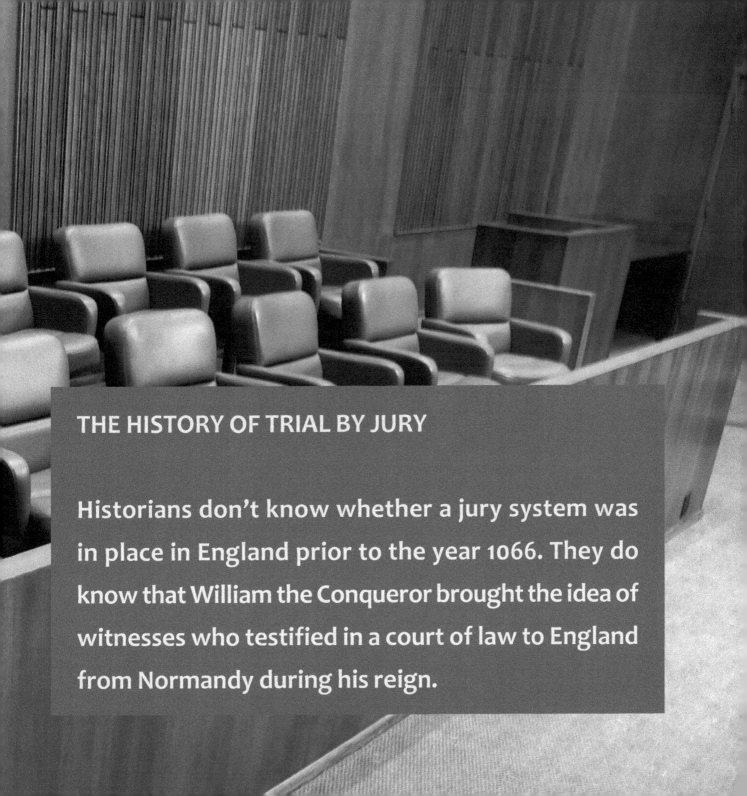

THE HISTORY OF TRIAL BY JURY

Historians don't know whether a jury system was in place in England prior to the year 1066. They do know that William the Conqueror brought the idea of witnesses who testified in a court of law to England from Normandy during his reign.

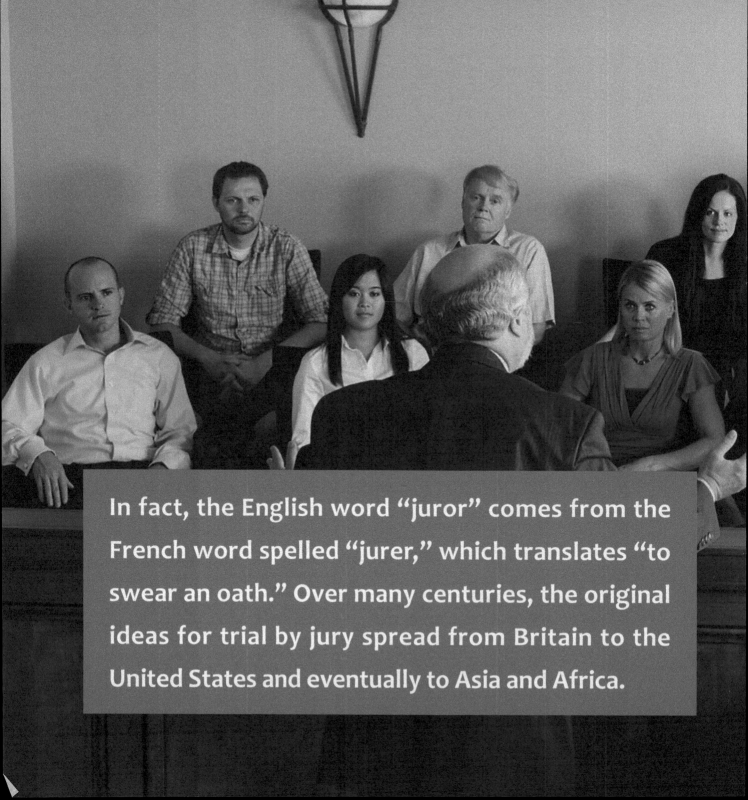

In fact, the English word "juror" comes from the French word spelled "jurer," which translates "to swear an oath." Over many centuries, the original ideas for trial by jury spread from Britain to the United States and eventually to Asia and Africa.

In the 12th century, the King of England used juries to help him make decisions about final rulings. The juries were designed to discover and state the facts in direct response to the questions the king asked. Although the juries presented evidence, only the king or trusted ministers were given the power to make final decisions.

It took three more centuries before jurors were to play a more important role. By the 15th century, the peer jury was at the core of English law. If you were on trial and you saw a jury member who was your sworn enemy, you could object to that person being part of the jury. It wasn't until the 17th century that a jury could really be honest about returning a verdict of either guilty or not guilty without some fear of consequences!

After the Revolutionary War, the system of jury duty became important to the American way of life. The right to a trial by peers meant that no king or dictator could decide an accused person's fate.

THE TYPES OF JURIES IN THE US COURT SYSTEM

The United States Constitution states that all citizens accused of crimes have the right to a trial by a jury of their peers. A jury is simply a group of people who determine whether the citizen being accused is guilty or not guilty.

There are two different types of juries. A grand jury is made up of sixteen to twenty-three jurors. The purpose of a grand jury is to determine whether an accusation is valid before a trial is held. A criminal petit jury or trial jury is the type of jury we think of when we think of "trial by jury." These juries consist of six to twelve individuals who determine whether the person or organization on trial is guilty or innocent in either a criminal or civil case.

Even though it may seem like an inconvenience to serve on a jury, 75% of all Americans believe that the jury system is the most impartial method of determining a person's guilt or innocence. Even federal judges have indicated that they would rather have a jury decide their fate rather than a lone judge if they were on trial.

WHO IS ELIGIBLE TO SERVE AS A JUROR?

In order to serve as a member of a jury you must be able to understand English and be at least 18 years of age. You can't have a felony on your record if you served in public office.

You would have to live within the court's jurisdiction and you can't be on active military duty since that is considered a priority. You can't also be part of another grand jury or trial jury. You can't be under a conservatorship, which simply means that you have someone else who manages your finances because you're not capable of doing so yourself.

You don't have to have a specific level of education or skill to be a juror.

Juries are composed of people from every background, social standing, and ethnicity. They are from all different walks of life and they are all ranges of ages, from 18 up.

HOW ARE POTENTIAL JURORS SELECTED?

You can't volunteer to be part of a jury. Jurors are randomly selected and notified by mail. The courts use lists that verify residency, lists of registered voters, and lists of individuals with driver's licenses or identification cards from which to pick potential jurors.

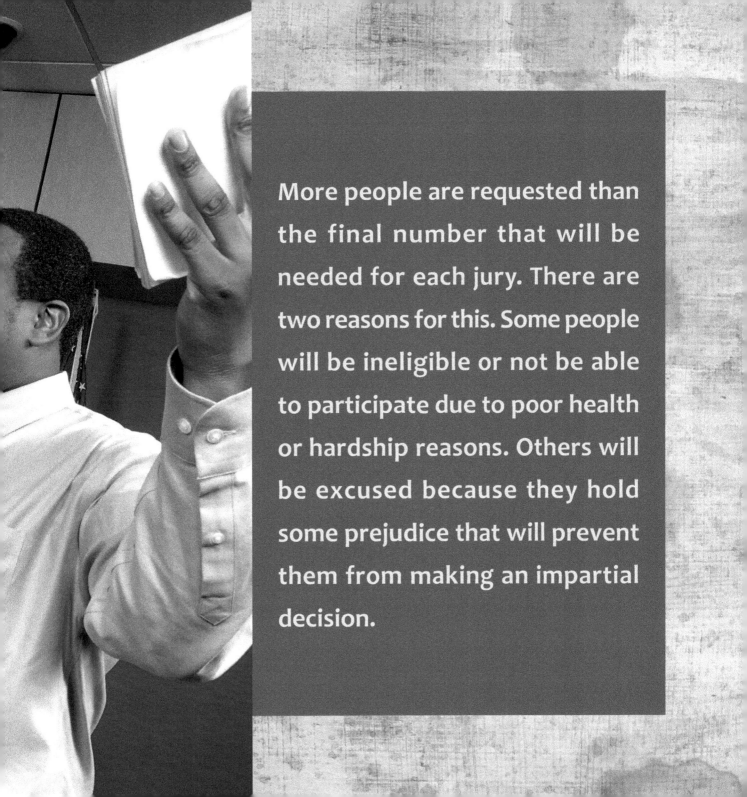

More people are requested than the final number that will be needed for each jury. There are two reasons for this. Some people will be ineligible or not be able to participate due to poor health or hardship reasons. Others will be excused because they hold some prejudice that will prevent them from making an impartial decision.

WHAT HAPPENS ONCE YOU'VE BEEN SUMMONED

Jury duty isn't voluntary. If you're summoned for jury duty, you must respond to let the court know if you will appear. If you can't for some hardship reason or you are ineligible, you must submit the reason and wait for the court to respond. If you don't appear without express permission from the court, you can be fined or sent to jail. Jury duty is every citizen's responsibility. After all, you would want a fair trial if you were being accused. In order to have fair trials, jurors are needed to perform this duty.

WHAT HAPPENS DURING
THE JURY SELECTION PROCESS?

The next stage of the process is the "voir dire," which means "true say" in Old French. The prospective jurors first report for duty. From that group, a panel is selected at random. That panel is sent to a specific courtroom and asked to repeat an oath that they will tell the truth. Then, the judge, as well as each attorney involved in the case, asks a series of questions to uncover whether a juror is impartial enough to listen to the evidence in the case. The judge may decide to excuse some individuals.

A judge can excuse a juror from service if he or she chooses to do so. If the judge feels that the juror will receive some financial benefit if the trial proceeds a certain way, then he or she might excuse the juror. Another reason might be because the individual has a bias that might make it impossible for him or her to think about the case fairly. If there has been a lot of media attention and the juror already feels strongly about whether the individual on trial is guilty or innocent, this might be a reason for dismissal. Another reason is if the potential juror has a family member who is related to someone who is involved in the case.

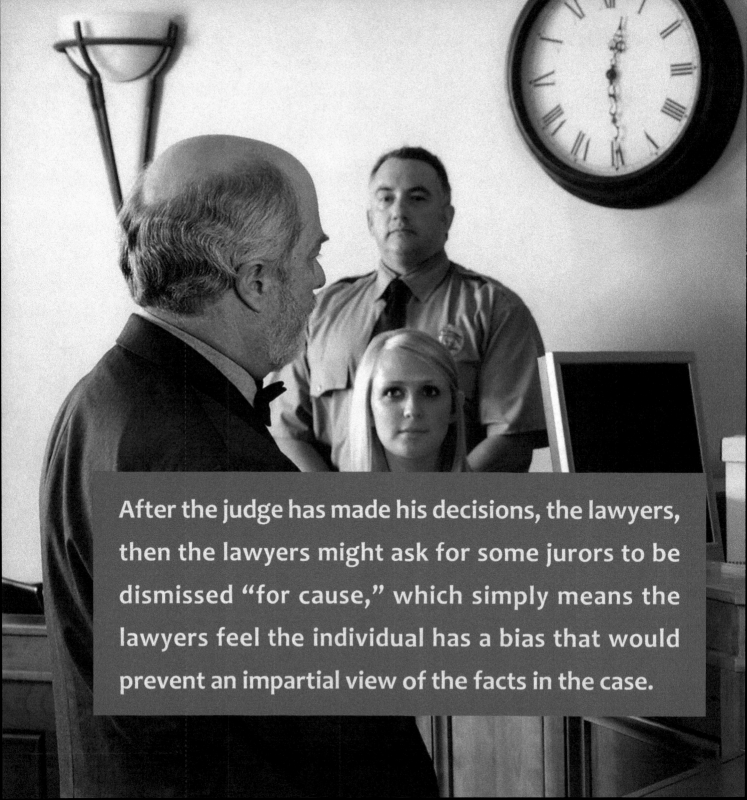

After the judge has made his decisions, the lawyers, then the lawyers might ask for some jurors to be dismissed "for cause," which simply means the lawyers feel the individual has a bias that would prevent an impartial view of the facts in the case.

PEREMPTORY CHALLENGES

In addition to being able to dismiss a juror "for cause," lawyers can also exercise "peremptory challenges." Each lawyer has a specific number of peremptory challenges and this essentially means that the lawyer can dismiss the juror based on a feeling that the juror won't serve the best interests of the lawyer's client. These peremptory challenges cannot be used to discriminate against the juror for any reason.

WHAT HAPPENS DURING A TRIAL

During a trial there can be unexpected happenings, but for the most part a typical trial follows this process:

If it's a criminal case, the prosecutor will state what he or she intends to prove and what evidence may be presented. If it's a civil case, the plaintiff's attorney will begin in a similar way.

The defense attorney sometimes prepares an opening statement as well.

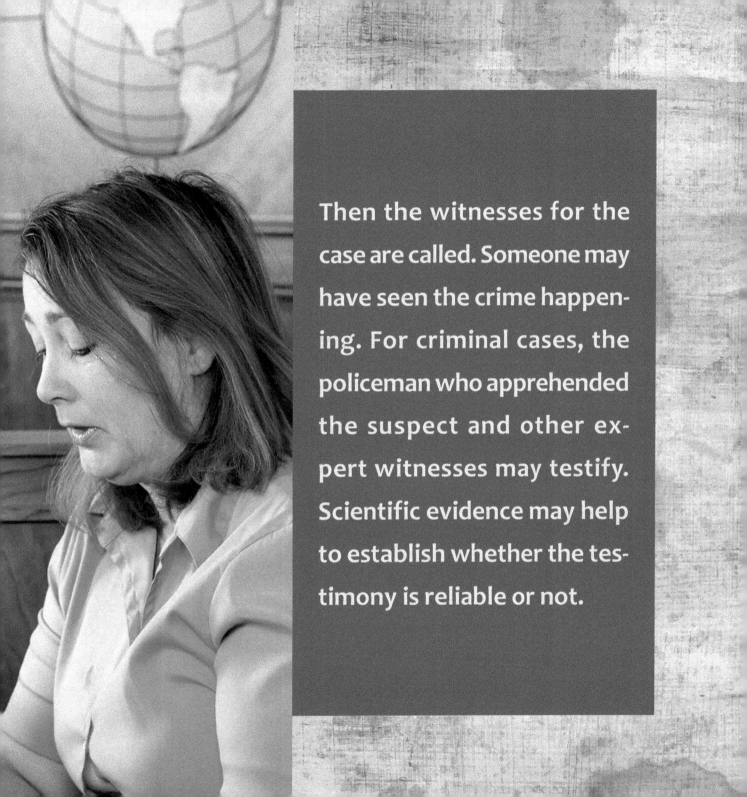

Then the witnesses for the case are called. Someone may have seen the crime happening. For criminal cases, the policeman who apprehended the suspect and other expert witnesses may testify. Scientific evidence may help to establish whether the testimony is reliable or not.

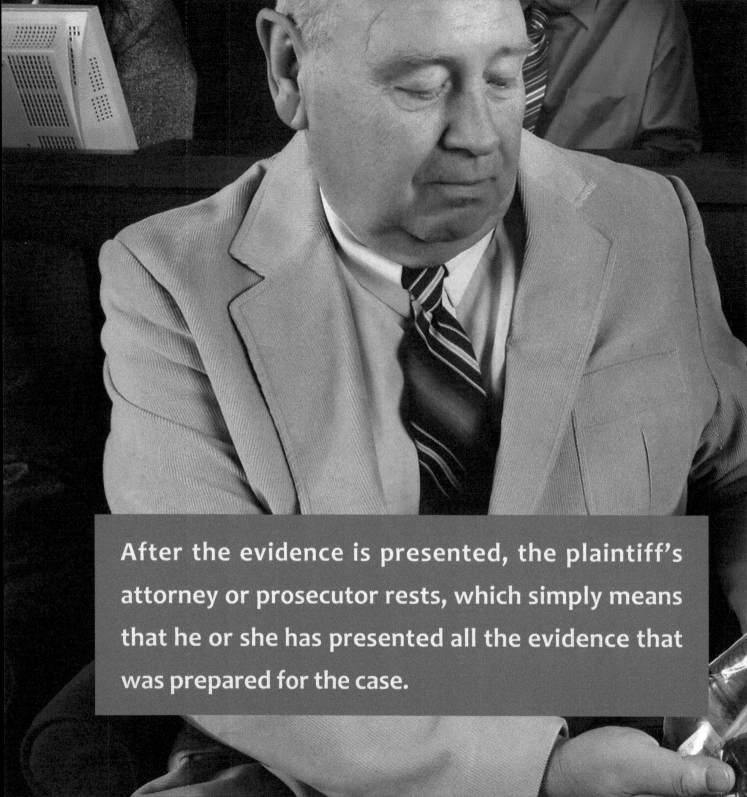

After the evidence is presented, the plaintiff's attorney or prosecutor rests, which simply means that he or she has presented all the evidence that was prepared for the case.

The defense attorney may offer evidence that puts the presentation of the opposite side in doubt. In our system of justice, the accused individual is assumed to be innocent unless there is no shadow of a doubt that the individual is guilty.

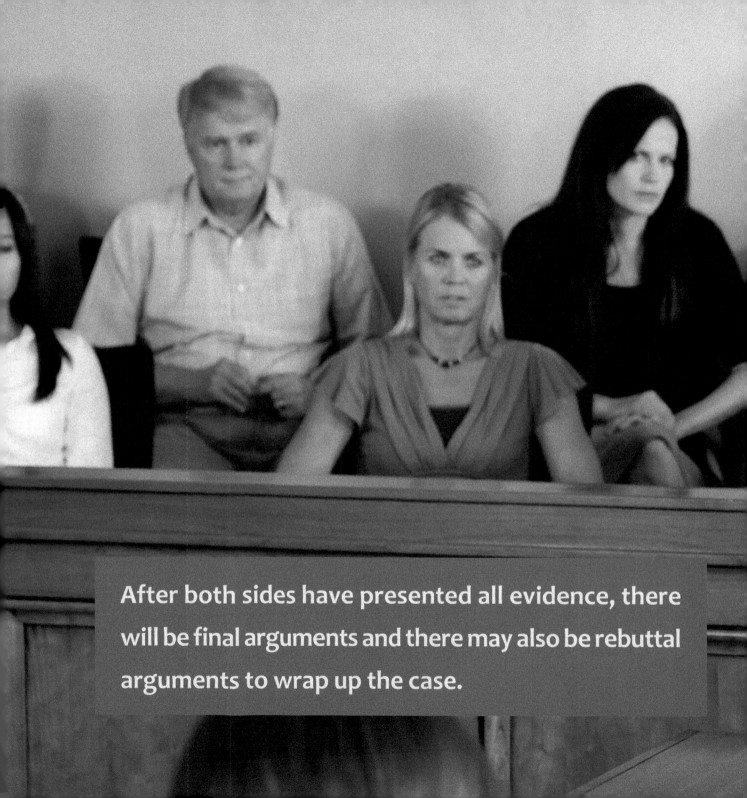

After both sides have presented all evidence, there will be final arguments and there may also be rebuttal arguments to wrap up the case.

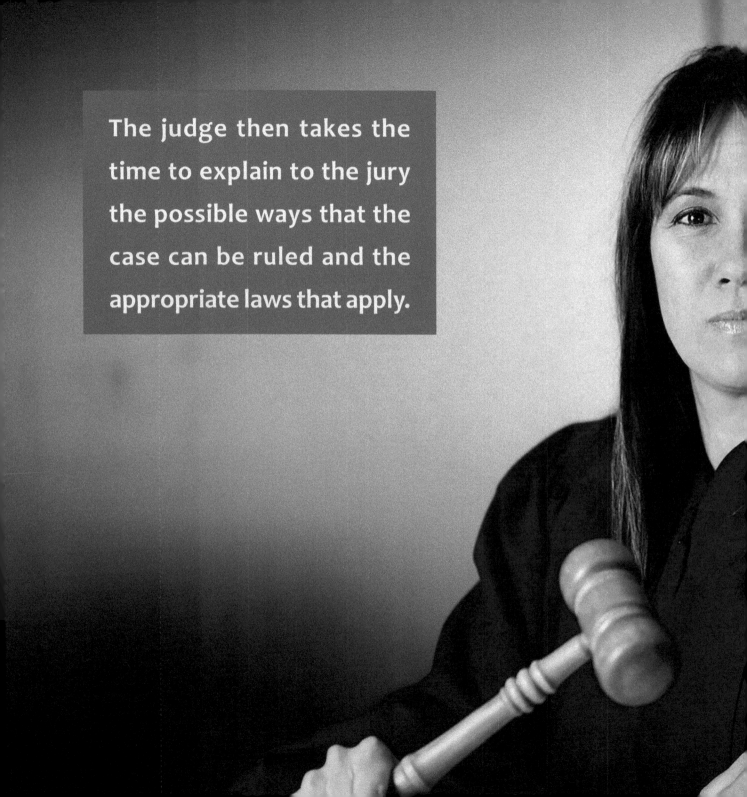

The judge then takes the time to explain to the jury the possible ways that the case can be ruled and the appropriate laws that apply.

For their final discussions and deliberations, the jury leaves the courtroom and goes into a separate jury room.

They choose a leader to communicate their decision. This leader is called the jury foreperson.

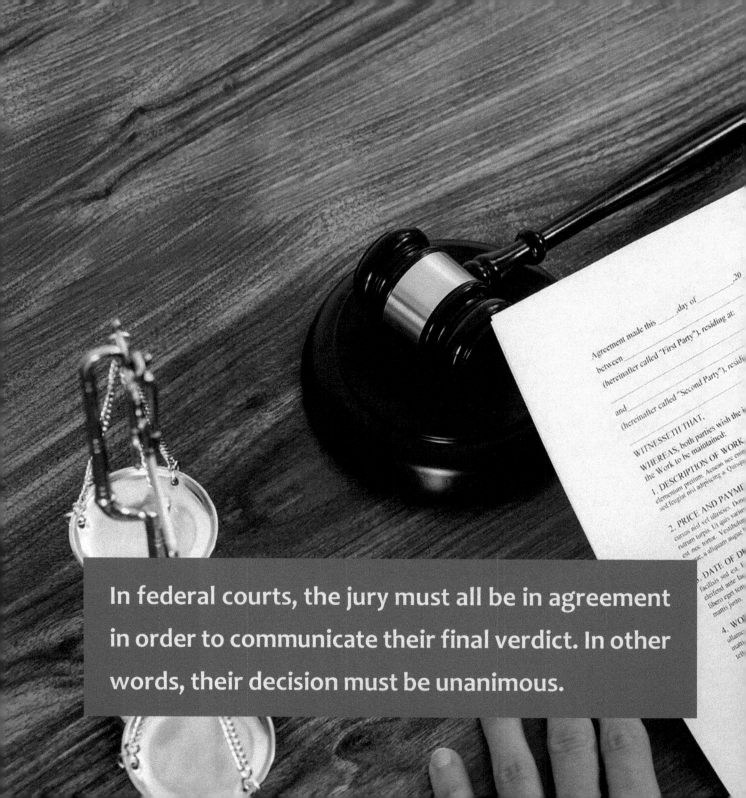

In federal courts, the jury must all be in agreement in order to communicate their final verdict. In other words, their decision must be unanimous.

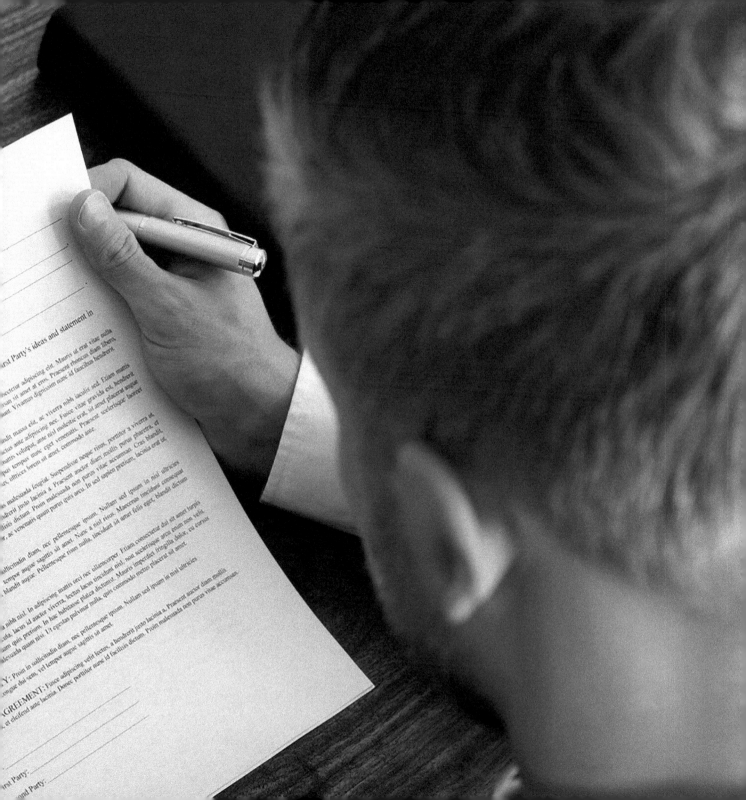

Awesome! Now you know jury duty is important so that courts can ensure that justice has been served. You can find more Government books from Baby Professor by searching the website of your favorite book retailer.

Visit

BABY PROFESSOR
EDUCATION KIDS

www.BabyProfessorBooks.com

to download Free Baby Professor eBooks
and view our catalog of new and exciting
Children's Books

Milton Keynes UK
Ingram Content Group UK Ltd.
UKHW050006300824
447530UK00002B/14